BRITAIN'S HERITAGE

1940s Fashion

Fiona Kay and Neil R. Storey

AMBERLEY

For Diane

First published 2018

Amberley Publishing
The Hill, Stroud
Gloucestershire, GL5 4EP

www.amberley-books.com

Copyright © Fiona Kay and Neil R. Storey, 2018

The right of Fiona Kay and Neil R. Storey to be identified as the Authors of this work has been asserted in accordance with the Copyrights, Designs and Patents Act 1988.

ISBN 978 1 4456 7915 0 (paperback)
ISBN 978 1 4456 7916 7 (ebook)

British Library Cataloguing in Publication Data.
A catalogue record for this book is available from the British Library.

Printed in the UK.

Contents

1

Introduction

The first half of the twentieth century saw some of the most dramatic changes in British women's fashions in modern history. Through the necessities of industrial working conditions and manual labour during the First World War, women said goodbye to restrictive corsetry and clothing. The generation of women who came after were able to enjoy the likes of trousers, looser fitting clothing and make-up like never before. Demand and competition in this burgeoning market drove on developments in fashion and cosmetic production that resulted in better quality items being made for more competitive prices and saw more women than ever before able to easily access fashionable clothes.

Thousands of sewing machines had been produced during the First World War for the manufacture of uniforms and equipment and the British sewing machine industry came on at such a pace that their prices came down and most households could now afford to buy their own machine outright, or at least be able to afford to rent or purchase one by monthly instalments. Women's magazines had included dressmaking patterns for years, enabling wealthy ladies to employ a dressmaker to make up just the item they desired. As the First World War progressed, patterns for women in practical jobs or in office work were published

'Carrying on ... in steel helmets.' Female workers in a north of England munitions plant pictured after they had been supplied with steel helmets to be worn by them when the 'alert' sounded or when the roof spotter warned against approaching aircraft, 1940.

Within the image (blackboard captions):

Fit + Swing
Nº 10,970
3½ yards 54 in. material
4 yards 36 in. lining

Edge to Edge Swagger
Nº 10,791
3½ yards 54 in. material
4¼ yards 36 in. lining

Appealing in Plaid
Nº 10,957
3½ yards 54 in. material
3½ yards 36 in. lining

A colour feature from *Woman's Own*, 9 March 1940. These are pre-Austerity designs for coats, displaying a longer length, fuller skirts and embellishments such as bows and edgings, all of which would be discouraged within two years. However, the distinctive square shoulders became a hallmark of the era.

The well-stocked Scotch Wool & Hosiery Stores, Shields Road, Newcastle, 1938. There were more than 350 branches of these stores throughout the UK, owned by the Worsted Mills of Fleming, Reid & Co., Greenock.

and more women started to make dresses in the home. The styles of the 1920s and '30s were far more simple and loose fitting than those of the Victorians and Edwardians and thus enabled more women to make clothing on home sewing machines.

Affordable fashions also became more and more prevalent on British high streets with pre-First World War companies such as Marks & Spencer (1884) and Dorothy Perkins (which began as H. P. Newman in 1909 but changed its trading name to Dorothy Perkins in 1919) creating off the peg fashionable clothes for women. Montague Burton (1903) and the Fifty Shilling Tailors (1905) came into their stride with chains of shops and their own factories making or, with major contracts, purchasing ready to wear fashionable suits for men from wholesale manufacturers at prices that would suit most pockets.

Cheap American imports of both clothing and cotton also helped to keep prices down, and as American films featuring glamorous ladies and snappily dressed men packed out the cinemas, more and more people became 'aware' of style and fashion and wanted to emulate screen stars. For women the likes of Rita Hayworth, Vivien Leigh and Dorothy Lamour, with their dressed hair and an air of elegance and femininity appealed. For the men it was the Spencer Tracy and James Cagney look, adopting fedoras, wider lapels and loose fitting trousers with turn-ups to give a more macho and edgy look to their 1930s styles.

All of this changed from the outbreak of war in September 1939. Imports were cut to the quick and stocks rapidly ran thin as people bought up what was left, fearing for the future

Workers at A. S. Wilkin's Cremona Toffee Works in Heaton, Newcastle, ready for a daytrip in 1938. The ladies are sporting an array of smart coats and hats and are carrying typical handbags of the time.

as factories switched to war production. The designs and fashions of the 1930s would linger on through the early years of the conflict, and as war gripped the nation, women wanted more than the out of date, worn out clothes they had been left with. So, with the economies necessitated by war and the restriction of coupons in mind, the Board of Trade and British designers had to work hand in hand to create something new and vivid for women in Utility clothing, lest the nation suffer the fall out of damaged morale among the women who were keeping the country going. How successful were they? Or did Britain just have to make do and mend its morale as well as its clothes during the Second World War?

This book does not pretend to be authoritative but we have drawn on decades of research and sifted through thousands of period magazines and newspapers, and, writing with the eyes of both a social and fashion historian, we present the story of those dark years when fashion really was on ration and what happened in the austere years afterwards to change the face of fashion yet again.

Fiona Kay and Neil Storey
2018

2
When War Broke Out

When the year 1939 opened, the British textile industry was enjoying a time where the public were looking to buy better value merchandise. The cheap overall cloth that had been so popular in the mid-1930s was out of favour and low-quality imported cottons were being replaced by an ever-growing demand for materials such as the versatile spun rayon, which held bold colours and designs well and was used in more dressy garments. If woven with wool, it also made a less expensive material than pure wool, ideal for everyday dresses and blouses. British manufacturers were also actively competing with American imported dresses by purchasing designs from the USA and making them from British-produced fabrics.

When war broke out on 3 September 1939, the U-boat menace instantly saw imports drop dramatically and prices for clothes, like those for tinned food, rose rapidly as people bought up stocks in fear of shortages caused by wartime circumstances. The War Risks Insurance Scheme was blamed by clothing manufacturers for the restriction in the supply of raw materials for civilian purposes enforced by the Government. Many manufacturers were also obliged by the newly created Ministry of Supply and Control to switch to war production, making uniforms, footwear and equipment for the expanding Army, Navy and Royal Air Force. The situation was further exacerbated by the National Service Act, introduced in 1939, which saw thousands of men lost from the workforce as they were called up (conscripted) for service in the fighting forces. Consequently, warehouse staff and delivery drivers became sparse, slowing down deliveries, and many firms had no other option than to begin rationing their orders.

Evacuees arriving at their new country school, 1939. As with preceding decades, children's fashions were simply smaller versions of adult clothes. Girls wore dresses and skirts and boys generally wore shorts, shirts and jackets, only donning longer trousers in their early teens. It was only in the late 1940s, with influences from America and their 'teenagers', that children's fashion started to separate from that of adults.

4057   7004   5055

An advert for Foster & Co. Ltd of Wood Street, London, 1939. The last fashion shows of 1939 occurred just before the outbreak of war. The fashions in this advert are influenced by those shows, with plenty of fabric, longer skirts and lots of embellishment. The square shoulders, a trademark of the 1940s, are already present.

The knee jerk reaction of the Government shortly after the outbreak of war of closing all places of entertainment, including dance halls and cinemas, along with the outburst of panic buying of clothes had the knock-on effect of new clothes, cosmetics and fancy hairstyles all being branded as 'unpatriotic' and 'counter-productive' to the war effort. Even shop opening hours were curtailed in densely populated areas deemed vulnerable to air attack and subject to stringent enforcement of the blackout. The *Sheffield Telegraph* of 14 September 1939 reported: 'Sheffield women are taking little or no interest in the new autumn fashions many drapers and coat and gown specialists in the city complain. The war appears to have filled women's minds with other considerations, and the necessity of buying a new outfit for the autumn has been thrust aside.'

It wasn't all doom and gloom on the fashion front. In a humorous article published in the *Daily Mirror* on 15 September 1939 headed 'Nazi Fashion News', they suggested: 'Since the Food Department has used up all available supplies of leather and the overfed British may cease to drop leaflets, boots are now being made of a rhubarb-leaf compound which, our experts assure us, is practically as good as anything ... Since the Fuhrer has decreed that trousers must be shorter, the tops of these boots are made especially high. We may safely predict that by this time next year trouser legs will practically have disappeared and that boots will be worn a little tight under the arms.'

This situation, however, could not be sustained for long because of its negative impact on morale. Those in authority had clearly not taken into consideration the fact that British people could endure most things with good humour and would be quite prepared to make their own decisions about taking the risk of gathering together in theatres, cinemas or dance halls to have a good time. Despite all that confronted it, the British manufacturing industry, including civilian clothing and textile makers, was determined to carry on hand in hand with the war effort. On 26 September 1939 Norman Hartnell staged the first major British fashion show in wartime in Mayfair,

This advert from S. Hubbard Ltd, published in *The Draper's Record* of September 1939, encourages everyone, including the hat and millinery trade, to keep morale up to ensure victory.

London. Presented were business-like day clothes with names like 'Soldier Boy', 'Air Force' and 'Good Shot' accessorised with matching gas mask carriers. The evening wear selection with wide hooped skirts and hobble skirts slit to the knee with names like 'Beautiful Spy' was greeted with acclaim. Hartnell proved it was possible to combine wartime expedients with the height of fashion and it was no surprise when he gained the Royal Warrant as Dressmaker to Queen Elizabeth the following year.

As the weeks and closing months of 1939 passed by, the war remained a very distant affair occurring on the Continent. The air raids that had been anticipated and feared for their 'knock out blows' against British cities and the ensuing thousands of casualties had simply not happened; indeed, what little German aerial action there was took place mainly over the seas just off our coastline with German aircraft on mine laying missions. As Christmas approached evacuees started to return home in droves and the situation became thought of as a 'Phoney War'. Hoarding was not encouraged over the first festive season of the war; there were certainly shortages but when it care to clothing high street stores urged people to 'Buy now while stocks

A studio portrait of a woman in a typical late 1930s coat, long and double-breasted with large patch pockets and a big turn-back collar, accessorised with large fur-backed gauntlets, a late 1930s style that lingered into the early years of the Second World War.

NOW!
more than ever

★ Now when you must economise a Singer Sewing Machine can save you pounds. You can make all your own garments and household requirements on a Singer and with the easy-to-use attachments obtain a real professional finish even on the most intricate stitching. Call at your local Singer shop for a FREE TRIAL—or write to Singer Sewing Machine Co. Ltd., Singer Building, City Road, London, E.C.1.

CASH OR CONVENIENT EASY TERMS

you need a

SINGER
sewing machine

HAND, TREADLE OR ELECTRIC MODELS

were still at the old prices', although people had to pause and give a bit more thought about their purchases, buying more practical and hard wearing clothes for their wardrobe. That said, people would have more time to stop and think as the British public encountered a phenomenon in shops like never before – the queue.

At home people began to mend their clothes and consider ways of making them last longer by reinforcing elbows and cuffs with leather, turning collars and patching and mending dresses where previously they may have thrown them away or handed them on. Children were more likely to be put in hand-me-down clothes or worn out or damaged adult clothes that were 'cut down' to fit, a process achieved with varying degrees of skill and success. A scheme created by the Women's Institute collected clothes and established clothing 'banks' to help meet the needs of evacuee children who rapidly outgrew their clothes.

The clothes shortages and wartime restrictions for adults and children alike resulted in the styles of the late 1930s lingering on as 'the look' of the early war years and throughout Britain's darkest hours in 1940.

An advert for Singer sewing machines, 1939. Home dressmaking had become popular in the previous decade; with the outbreak of war and the subsequent rationing scheme, it became almost a necessity. Despite reduced production during the war (the Singer plant was switched to the production of munitions), Singer remained one of the most popular brands of machine.

3
When the Siren Wailed

The first air raid siren sounded on the day war broke out; it was a false alarm, but the long-held fear of air attack had a profound effect on wartime fashions.

The introduction of National Service, conscripting men of a serviceable age and set criteria from the outset of the war (conscription for women was introduced in December 1941), meant the notion of being seen to be doing something for the war effort became de rigueur. Personnel in military uniforms became a common sight on British streets. Established pre-war organisations such as the British Red Cross Society and St John Ambulance Brigade had some stocks of uniforms to outfit their new members, but their stocks were soon depleted, and many members resorted to wearing a simple armband on their civilian clothes. The women who volunteered for ambulance driving were kitted out with long coats of woollen greatcoat material, a cap, tin helmet and gas mask. This was a uniform they liked because it was easy to don at any time of the day if they were called. Many of these girls would recall how they attended emergencies after being called from their beds in the dead of night, driving their ambulances wearing a pair of wellies and their night attire under their greatcoat. The new

A group of air raid wardens, photographed early in the war when their 'uniform' consisted of a tin helmet, an armband and a lapel badge. The men are all wearing pre-Utility suits, some double-breasted, and there are turn ups on the trousers, pocket flaps and waistcoats; all of these would be banned under the austerity measures.

Newly recruited lady ambulance drivers, 1940. Some of them wear the typical coats and hats that provided their first uniforms, worn over their civilian clothes, while others have to make do with armbands until their uniforms arrive.

A volunteer canteen worker proudly wearing her Women's Voluntary Service Civil Defence badge, 1940.

wartime organisations of 1939 such as the Air Raid Wardens, Auxiliary Fire Service, and Women's Voluntary Service (WVS) were not so fortunate. Initially, they had no uniforms apart from painted tin helmets and boiler suits or overalls worn when on duty, so armbands and lapel badges became important features on wartime civilian clothing to show the wearer was doing his or her 'bit'.

Shops and businesses advertising in magazines and newspapers were quick to cotton on to the new markets generated by Air Raid Precautions. Among the first of these products was the gas mask case or cover. Gas masks were first issued back in 1938, after the Munich Crisis. Contained in neat, stiff cardboard boxes, there was no legal requirement to carry them, although it was encouraged extensively in the press. Poster campaigns urged 'Hitler will send no warning. Always carry your gas mask', while some social venues like cinemas, theatres and dance halls refused admittance if the customer was not carrying one. The problem was that if they were carried at all times, the boxes and strings soon wore out and if they got wet the box was often ruined. So the gas mask cover was introduced. They could be made to patterns at home, decorated or bought commercially in every imaginable material from Gabardine to leather. A number of impromptu gas mask drills caught women out with their gas masks in the bottom of their handbags, causing an array of handbag contents and precious make-up containers to spill all over the pavement, creating trip hazards. As a result gas mask handbags, dedicated to making the gas mask easily accessible, and including pockets for other items such as purses and make-up, were created.

From the earliest days of the war women had started buying more practical clothing such as warm dressing gowns, house coats and knitwear to be worn if the family had to decamp to a cold air raid shelter down the garden or in the street. With blackouts enforced across the country, street lights were turned off and there was a huge increase in accidents caused by poor visibility in the darkened streets. Consequently, kerbs, corners of buildings, door frames and street obstacles such as trees, lamp posts and bollards had white bands

In the early war years lapel badges were worn to signify that those not in military uniforms were 'doing their bit'. The badge of the AFS (Auxiliary Fire Service) can be seen clearly on this gentleman's lapel.

painted on them and people had to think carefully about how they could be seen in the blackout. A whole range of white and luminous items soon hit the market. There were buttons and circular button badges and flower brooches to be worn in the lapels of jackets and coats, white armbands, umbrella covers, white pixie hoods, handbags, belts, luminous waistcoats, hatbands, armbands, belts, crossbands and walking sticks.

Lapel badge worn by volunteers in the Auxiliary Fire Service. Introduced in August 1938, this badge was originally issued to signify that the wearer had completed sixty hours' training. The qualification time was reduced to one month and members' badges were made in white metal from June 1939.

Left: Weldon's Ladies' Journal, April 1940. Dressmaking patterns in women's magazines had been popular throughout the preceding two decades. The outbreak of war increased their importance as restrictions started to bite. Home embellishment of garments became popular and patriotic designs abounded. This magazine had 'Jolly Jack Tars', 'Service Badges' and 'Good Luck Motifs' on offer among its embroidery transfers.

Below: The black-out created a new market for fabrics and products to be seen in the dark. This advert from Charles Taylor of Leeds for 'Reliable' goods dating from 1939 covers a number of such items.

THANK GOODNESS
MINER'S LIQUID MAKE-UP
STAYS MATT—ALWAYS !

We hope you'll never have to mask your beauty — but if you do, remember there's one make-up that stays matt whatever happens — and that's Henry C. Miner's wonderful Liquid Make-up. Smooth it on — and you've got a silken-soft, fine-textured, delicately-tinted and perfumed complexion that stays put through blackouts, business rushes, air-raid alarms, seeing him off . . . and welcoming him home again. Remember the name of this wartime wizardry — it's

HENRY C. MINER'S

Liquid Make-up

In 6 skin-toning shades, 1/3. Trial size 6d

STAYS MATT WHATEVER HAPPENS!

Don't take war to bed with you!

WEAR LOVELY
FERGUSON FABRICS
SEWN WITH
SAVING
SENSE

Go TO BED every night in the peace-time luxury of Ferguson's lovely lingerie fabrics. And should the syren sound, this clever pyjama suit jumps into slacks and sweater in a trice. The fabric is gay, pretty, printed Juliesyl. The sleeves and smartly gathered trouser legs are comfortingly draught-excluding ! ! Moreover, Ferguson's Juliesyl still only costs you 3/3 a yard and it washes and wears so beautifully. Sewn with saving sense. Ferguson Fabrics are really a wonderful wartime economy.

A FERGUSON FABRIC

FERGUSON BROS. LTD.   HOLME HEAD WORKS, CARLISLE

Above Left: After the First World War it became more and more acceptable for women to wear make-up daily. Despite initial feelings that worrying about make-up and the way you look was unpatriotic, it was soon acknowledged that it was essential for morale and adverts such as this one used this as a selling point. *Above Right:* The siren suit was a practical solution to night time air raid sirens. It kept you looking respectable and was warm. You could either pull your jumper and trousers on over the top or slip on your winter coat and you were ready to go.

More outlandish ideas included large white gauntlet gloves, exaggerated berthe collars going from neck to shoulders and even large white inserts down the side seam of trousers. As the war progressed and limited lighting was allowed on some signage and in specific places (which was to be extinguished immediately if the sirens sounded), most people took to carrying a newspaper or wearing a white scarf or lighter coloured coat when they were out and about in the dark.

Even though many people carried on just wearing their ordinary night attire with a few extra layers and a coat in easy reach in case of an air raid, one garment above all others has become synonymous with wartime home front clothing – the siren suit. Based on the designs of pre-war one-piece ski clothing, siren suits and so-called ARP suits of a similar ilk soon made their appearance. As one advert proclaimed:

> The need for a comfortable, convenient, warm and quick-to-slip-on A.R.P. Suit has been met by Jersey Fabrics Ltd., Albert Mills, Gamble Street, Nottingham, who have devised a really attractive article which has been duly patented and placed on the market. The fact that the suit, which is on the zip principle and can be donned in a few seconds, is exposure proof and suitable for men, women and children should readily commend itself. Known as the "A.R.P. Alarm suit," the article has been patented in all fabrics, and should meet a distinct need, especially for those who have to dress hurriedly.

There were soon suits for both adults and children. Made in various designs and colours including soft grey flannel with scarlet cuffs, tab pockets and hood lining, flannel in scarlet and emerald on grey with plain scarlet facings, gaberdine, wool twill and tweed, some were even fleece lined and came with mittens attached. Siren suits caught the public's imagination,

Child's Hooded SIREN SUIT *(2-3 years)*

BESTWAY LEAFLET No. 446

3d

Knit your children their own siren suit, complete with the latest fad, the Pixie hat. Patterns like these were enormously popular and were available both over the counter from drapers and in women's magazines.

featuring in the national media. When Princess Juliana of the Netherlands was evacuated to Britain on 13 May 1940, they arrived at Liverpool Street station and it was reported that her eldest daughter, two-year-old Princess Beatrix, was clad in a siren suit. Siren suits were soon advertised and commented on in fashion features as becoming popular for evenings at home as 'lounging pyjamas'. The 'onesie' is nothing new!

> The most famous wearer of siren suits was wartime Prime Minister Winston Churchill. He had several made in a variety of materials, including green velvet, but preferred to call them his 'romper-suits'. In 2002 one of his surviving grey pinstripe suits sold at auction for £30,000.

Both national and provincial newspapers included Home Front necessities in their competitions. The *Nelson Leader* in August 1940 offered a handsome first prize for their literary competition consisting of £100 cash, plus a lady's siren suit, an ARP hamper (containing a bottle each of whisky and brandy, tinned goods and 100 cigarettes), and a hamper for a member of HM Forces. 'We are sure the winner Miss Muriel Arnold of Burnley would have put all the items to good use'.

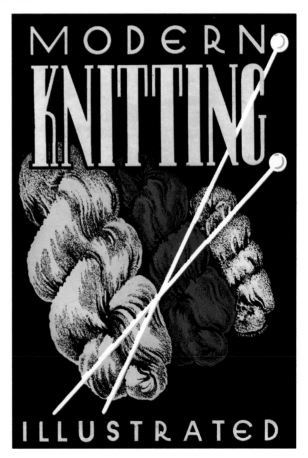

Cover of the book *Modern Knitting*, which contained a host of home knit patterns that became popular in wartime Britain.

One pursuit predominantly adopted by women on the Home Front in wartime was knitting. It was suggested as something women and girls could do down in the shelter during the air raid to pass the time away productively and it became a phenomenal success as it could be done during just about any spare moment. The government issued wool and knitting needles to schools and set up programmes to teach children how to knit. Special stocks of wool were

supplied to Women's Institutes and issued freely for the knitting of forces garments. Knitting circles were formed as offshoots from a host of organisations from churches and religious groups to war workers, and local communities made thousands of garments from socks and scarves to balaclavas and gloves for the services. Local newspapers and journals such as *Home and Country* published the contributions of local branches and groups with pride; some of the amounts of knitwear produced by these groups every month was remarkable. For women with family commitments or who were too old to serve in other ways, this to them was their 'war work'. During the course of the war the Women's Institutes of England & Wales sent over 22 million knitted garments to the Red Cross to be distributed to the armed forces. If you had a little bit of time for yourself, you might just be able to run up a jumper out of scraps.

Above & Opposite: Knitting for the services became a very popular pastime. Numerous patterns were available for items deemed essential for the Army, Navy and Air Force and even the Home Front services. Although knitting wool was rationed for personal use, there was a certain amount of carefully controlled wool available from the WVS for service garments. It was carefully noted how much you received to ensure the same amount was returned in knitted form.

4
Battle Dress

When war broke out, the Ministry of Supply and Control was armed with the necessary powers to ensure that the major clothing and footwear manufacturers of Great Britain switched to Government contracts and entered into war production of uniforms, equipment, boots and shoes. The factories of Montague Burton, one of the country's largest high street gentleman's outfitters, made a quarter of all the British uniforms during the Second World War. The Fifty Shilling Tailors made uniforms too, as did a panoply of other independent wholesale factories like F. W. Harmer of Norwich, J. Compton, Son & Webb, Town Tailors Ltd,

SPRING MODES

In 1940 Ernest Bevin was appointed the Minister for Labour and National Service, responsible for the country's labour force and the allocation of manpower. This cartoon, which first appeared in the satirical magazine *Punch* on 26 March 1941, shows him with a window display of uniforms worn by women in the services at the time. Conscription for women was introduced in December that same year.

Denhams (1933) Ltd, Harry Levine Ltd of London, William Templeton & Sons, J. & J. Mendes Ltd, Bairstow, Sons & Co. Ltd, M. Belmont & Co. and even the Dunlop Rubber Co. Ltd to name but a few. Most of these factories produced wool serge battledress jackets and trousers – the durable, disposable and interchangeable standard kit for the fighting forces. When first issued it would look like the proverbial 'sack of spuds' but with pressing and some work by the company tailors, it could look quite smart and provided the operational kit for the Army, RAF air crew, Royal Marines and some arms of the Royal Navy during the war. The Home Guard were also issued battledress from late 1940, as were the Civil Defence and Observer Corps from 1941.

> Approximately one third of the population of Great Britain were entitled to wear a uniform during the Second World War – 15 million people, almost a third of which served in the armed forces.

When this image first appeared in 1941, it was criticised for being too glamorous and, according to Conservative MP Thelma Cazalet, misrepresenting 'the rigours of Army life'. The government eventually gave in and created a series of posters showing photographic images of actual members of the ATS working in their roles as despatch riders and drivers.

BURBERRY
R.A.F. KIT

Undergraduates and other gentlemen intending to take up permanent or short service commissions in the Royal Air Force are advised to apply to Burberrys Ltd. (appointed outfitters to the Royal Air Force College) for particulars and prices of Kit.

Burberry representatives visit all Air Stations in England to meet the convenience of customers.

Well-known men's clothiers such as Burberry, Moss Bros and Burtons became leading suppliers of tailored uniforms to officers of Britain's fighting forces.

Battledress, although iconic for the fighting man, could never match for style and finesse the well-tailored British Army and RAF officers' four-pocket Officer Service Dress uniforms, in green and blue barathea respectively with polished brass buttons, or the Royal Navy officer's reefer jacket and trousers in navy blue barathea with gilt buttons. It should be remembered, however, that these were not issued as items of uniform and the majority of them would have been made to measure at an independent high street tailors or by quality chains such as Alkit Ltd, Flights Ltd or Burberry. There was a small subsidy but the majority of the purchase of this uniform and associated accoutrements would have been paid for out of the pocket of the officer himself. Many tailors realised this and, not wishing to lose the trade, offered terms for payment over a set number of instalments.

Women's military services, specifically the Auxiliary Territorial Service (ATS) and Women's Auxiliary Air Force (WAAF), were also supplied with thousands of factory made uniforms. Their design was based on a fashionable militaristic walking suit of 1939. The material they were made from was of a finer wool composition and all women in the ATS and WAAF were issued four-pocket jackets with brass buttons to polish. Just like the men, the women would also have their uniforms officially tailored and they were not above shortening the skirts and putting in a few more discreet darts here and there to complement their figure.

The Wrens' jacket was different to the other two services. Plans had been made when the Wrens were reformed shortly before the war for a finer fabric than the pusser's serge used in the First World War; however, supply became difficult and the only thing to use was regular navy serge. The idea of a sailor collar outfit was discussed but the idea was unpopular and they ended up with double-breasted jackets with black plastic buttons bearing the standard Royal Navy crown and fouled anchor. All female officers, regardless of service, had to purchase their service dress uniforms just like the men; often the tailors local to female officers' training centres would employ and train female staff to attend and measure up the

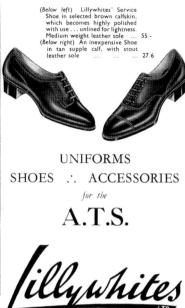

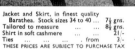

Jacket and Skirt, in finest quality
  Barathea. Stock sizes 34 to 40 ... 7½ gns.
Tailored to measure ... ... 8½ gns.
Shirt in soft cashmere 21/-
Ties ... ... from 3/-
THESE PRICES ARE SUBJECT TO PURCHASE TAX

Greatcoat in best quality Melton
  cloth. Stock sizes 34 to 40 ... 9½ gns.
Tailored to measure ... 10½ gns.
Hat in felt, including Badge ... 35/-
THESE PRICES ARE SUBJECT TO PURCHASE TAX

Women could also obtain tailored uniforms from well-known clothiers, such as Lillywhites Ltd. The latter offered a full service supplying not only the uniforms but appropriate footwear and accessories.

Six members of the Auxiliary Territorial Service (ATS) attached to the Royal Artillery (Anti-Aircraft Command) in the north of England, October 1941. They wear the four-pocket tunic and display a variety of the hairstyles popular among female service personnel at the time. As you can see, some have worked better when worn under a hat than others.

Above Left: An Aircraftswoman Second Class, Women's Auxiliary Air Force, c. 1941. Her uniform mirrors the four pockets with fabric belt and brass buckle and buttons of the ATS but in RAF blue.
Above Right: A member of the Royal Observer Corps wearing her woollen battledress top, c. 1944.

female officers and a few of the well-respected high street names such as Lillywhites and Moss Bros offered a similar service by appointment.

The most significant difference between the uniforms worn by male and female service personnel of all ranks in all three of these women's military services was that women were issued with a skirt. Fortunately, there were overalls for women engaged in work that would require them. It was only from 1941 that the ATS and the WAAF started to see women's designed battledress jackets and trousers issued as standard working kit. The Wrens are occasionally seen wearing bell-bottomed sailor's trousers if their trade or working conditions demanded them, but in the main they remained in skirts.

In 1942, however, the hat for WRNS ratings changed. They had been wearing a modernised version of the original 'pudding basin' hat from 1918, which was based on a Bond Street yachting hat. This had proved very unpopular because it was difficult to look smart in it; indeed, the then First Lord of the Admiralty Mr A. V. Alexander, backed by admirals, insisted on change. The year 1942 saw the sailor's cap introduced and it was so popular that it became the hallmark of the WRNS and was soon copied among the latest civilian fashions in a variety of colours and materials.

A 'uniform' for the WVS began with simple wrap-around overalls in the distinctive WVS green colour in 1939. A full, business-like uniform had been the idea of Lady Reading, the founder of the WVS, who managed to persuade London couturier Digby Morton to design a suit, blouse and overcoat 'as a matter of public duty'. Initially, it was available to any member on production of their badge at a number of good-quality high street retailers around the country for the grand sum of 55s. Regulations were soon changed and permits

Above Left: In 1942 the sailor's cap was introduced to the Women's Royal Naval Service (WRNS). It became so popular that it not only became the hallmark of the WRNS but sparked an immediate civilian fashion among young women, who could purchase one in a variety of colours and materials. *Above Right*: A female officer in the Auxiliary Fire Service (AFS) wearing the dress side hat popular with both military and civil women's services c. 1940.

had to be obtained from the local WVS Centre leader at Headquarters to purchase the outfit. A lighter weight uniform dress by Lillywhites of London was launched in 1940 and a distinctive green beret followed in January 1941. The WVS was always practical about uniform; their regulations stated 'WVS members in responsible positions, and especially those in contact with the civil authorities are asked to wear uniform when on official business', but there was no obligation for its working members to wear one, just the badge and overalls, when doing their invaluable work in rest centres and canteens.

The Women's Land Army, although not a fighting force, worked hard on the land in all weathers. Day to day most of the girls worked in their issue dungarees and a mix of their officially issued jumpers and their own, the approved and non-approved shirts or blouses and a pair of wellies if necessary. If they were in their

A British Red Cross Society Voluntary Aid Detachment member, c. 1941.

Above Left: Advertisers used both military and Home Front female services to patriotically advertise goods, as can be seen here in this 1944 avert for Kolynos Dental Cream, which advertises itself as essential to the nation's health in the same way the WVS is essential to the war effort.

Above Right: Members of the Women's Land Army make the cover of *Home Notes*, October 1944. Vita Sackville-West advised: 'You cannot look fashionable in uniform; you can usually look only trim, neat and correct; but the Land Girls uniform does offer the alternative of looking picturesque.'

Despite limitations on fabric availability, suppliers still encouraged women to purchase when possible. Here, Sparva Fabrics uses the routine of a woman's life in uniform as a contrast to the brightness of their fabrics.

Put your best face forward . . .

War jobs leave little time for beauty ritual, but good looks and good

morale go hand in hand. So make up your mind to put your best face

forward every day; to see that your mirror reflects your faith in victory.

Yardley Bond Street Complexion Powder gives you a natural loveliness

that is completely in the picture nowadays. And its delicate perfume

is perfectly attuned to our new ways of life.

If you have any wartime beauty problems write to Mary Foster, the Yardley Beauty consultant. She will be very glad to help you.

★ *With tax, Yardley Complexion Powder costs 4/-. Look for the familiar packing, but remember that though Yardley beauty-things sometimes wear wartime dress, they still have all the qualities you know and trust.*

YARDLEY · 33 OLD BOND STREET · LONDON W1

An advert for Yardley 'Bond Street' face powder, *Britannia and Eve*, 1 July 1943. Make-up became more difficult to come by as the war progressed, although this did not stop manufacturers producing advertising campaigns using the glamour of Hollywood or the perceived glamour of the women's services to sell their goods.

'full dress', out and about on the street or on parade, they had a green jumper, cream aertex shirt, a WLA issue tie and armband, an enamelled metal badge (worn on the jumper or the hat), corduroy breeches, tall socks and leather shoes, a smart hat and even a greatcoat designed by Worth. Vita Sackville-West wrote: 'You cannot look fashionable in uniform; you can usually look only trim, neat and correct; but the Land Girls uniform does offer the alternative of looking picturesque.'

War paint

Girls working in ordnance factories needed to wear protective foundation to preserve their skin from chemicals. In 1942 shortages became so severe that the Ministry of Supply issued workers with an allowance for the high-grade foundation and face powder. It was thick and unpleasant but had a slight tint.

Women in both the military and civilian forces (apart from the Red Cross and St John Ambulance) were usually permitted to wear subtle make-up; painted fingernails were not permitted but face and hand creams, face powder and lipsticks were often stocked in their canteens. Uniformed female service personnel frequently featured in adverts for cosmetics and some brands extolled the virtues of their products in advertising with servicewomen in mind. Firms like Cyclax, for example, produced 'Auxiliary Red' lipstick and rouge available in service beauty kits to fit uniform pockets. Adverts for Tangee Natural lipstick advised uniformed women: 'On duty you must look smart – but never painted.' An article attributed to the NAAFI reproduced in a number of magazines and newspapers claimed: 'The A.T.S like red lipstick to tone with their khaki. W.A.A.F.'s like the blue-red petunia shades and the W.R.N.S prefer a fairly bright pure scarlet to brighten up the dark blue.' The sentiments of the times were summed up in the oft-repeated slogan of 'Beauty – It's your duty.'

'Beauty is a duty' became something of a rallying call during the Second World War. All women, no matter whether they were in the Forces, Land Army or working in a factory, were expected to take care of their appearance.

5
Fashion on the Ration

Shortages and restriction on clothing were anticipated as part and parcel of wartime conditions from the outbreak of war in 1939, a situation summed up in a report published in *The Journal* of 27 September 1939: 'It is up to designers and manufacturers to style for artistic utility and to avoid garishness and extravagance. I am sure that they will see to it that women will look their best under all conditions.'

By February 1940 consumption of wool was up 30 per cent on the peak of demand during the First World War and after more imports had been hit by enemy action, notably the sinking of two cargo ships containing wool for the UK by the *Graf Spee*, wool prices rose to 70 per cent more than before the outbreak of war. Matters did not improve as the war progressed. As raw materials became increasingly scarce they commanded inflated prices that forced up the price of clothes, and the introduction of a purchase tax in October 1940 of between 33 and a third per cent and 100 per cent on garments (for luxuries like fur) didn't help. By April 1941 clothes prices had risen to 72 per cent above their 1939 level. The situation was not sustainable and there were rumblings among the population and popular press about the disparity between the 'haves' and the 'have nots'.

The rationing of clothes was introduced on 1 June 1941. Its introduction has been described as 'the best kept secret of the war' – initially there were not even any special clothing ration books printed and extra margarine coupons were to be used instead. There had been no warning announcements as they would almost certainly have led to another spree of panic buying that would have made shortages even more acute. Racketeers would

 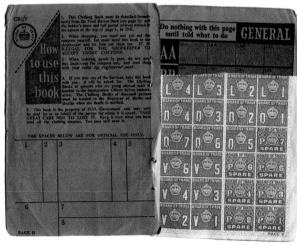

The first round of clothing rationing started on 1 June 1941, when everyone was given sixty-six coupons. By the time this book was issued in 1944 the allowance had fallen to forty-six.

Supporting the War Effort

The corset industry soon found that the steel used in corsets was not classed as an 'essential' and corsets became floppy, not providing the required support. Women in the services and other roles that meant often having to stand for long hours became vocal about the need for good supporting corsetry. The Corset Guild of Great Britain was formed in 1943 by retail shop buyers and leading corset manufacturers. In early 1944 they presented a petition to 10 Downing St on behalf of British women regarding the need for supporting corsetry. As a result, in March 1944 corsetry was classified under the 'Essential Works Order', enabling manufacturers to maintain certain standards and produce garments that were capable of being both comfy and providing the required back support.

Such clever clothes!

Coupon-canny wardrobe team! Tailored Utility blouse in washable rayon crêpe. White, sky, pink, peach or turquoise. 3 sizes; 17/9. Four coupons. Fine woollen skirt with follow-my-leader pleats all around. Waist sizes 24, 26, 28, 30. Black, navy, tobacco, wine; 39/11. Grey 45/-. Six coupons. Variety show of other styles to choose from!

RICHARD SHOPS

13, BANK PLAIN · NORWICH

This advert for Richard Shops in Norwich is an interesting mix of Utility and non-Utility clothing. The blouse is clearly advertised as a Utility item but the skirt with its 'follow-my-leader pleats all around' falls well outside of Utility restrictions, and the customer would probably have had to spend a decent amount of money on top of their coupons to purchase it.

also have bought up goods for the black market. It was simple: the people of Great Britain woke up on the morning of 1 June 1941 to find clothes rationing was now mandatory.

Initially clothes rationing used the twenty-six 'spare' coupons at the back of the food ration book, plus an additional forty issued on a green card at a later date (the first official issue of clothing ration books was made in 1942). The price of an article made no difference to coupon value. When buying new clothes, the shopper had to hand over coupons with a 'points' value as well as money. This meant that wealthier customers could still obtain their better quality clothes, but as the *Sunday Mirror* pointed out: 'One suit for the millionaire and one suit for the peasant!' and 'They may be able to eat smoked salmon and roast chicken at the Savoy but they will only be able to buy one suit a year, just the same as the labourer in Wigan.' It was illegal to sell spare coupons but there was soon a thriving trade in spare, stolen and forged clothing coupons on the black market.

Among the clothing now rationed were: woollen dresses and skirts, stockings, cami-knickers, men's suits, cotton shirts, shoes, elastic, vests, corsets and knickers. Leather was rationed as it was needed

Above Left: A pair of new shoes would cost you five precious coupons from your annual allowance and you'd probably buy only one pair a year, if that. Consequently, the pair you purchased needed to be long lasting.

Above Right: *Stitchcraft,* November 1941. *Stitchcraft* was a popular magazine of the time. As the war went on, it contained more articles on how to eke out limited wool and fabric supplies for both clothing and household linens; for example, how to use fabric scraps to create the very popular turban.

to make footwear for service personnel, so women's shoes were made from the likes of fabric, raffia, canvas, gabardine and plaited straw and had cork soles and heels because rubber was also in short supply. Production of silk stockings was banned in 1940 and the material was substituted with rayon, cotton and wool. Women often chose to wear knee length and ankle socks instead or infamously used to paint their legs with gravy browning to affect a tanned stocking look, some even going so far as to draw a seam up the back of their legs with an eyebrow pencil. Items not rationed included: hats and caps, sewing thread, mending wool, shoelaces, tapes, braids and ribbons under 3 inches wide, braces, clogs, blackout cloth, household linen, umbrellas and second-hand clothes.

Working clothes wore out as ever and workers found it hard to replace them, so in September 1942 it was announced that 'millions of workers in a great variety of trades' were to receive ten extra clothing coupons during the current rationing period. Called the 'Industrial Ten',

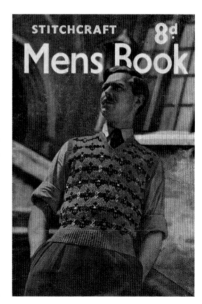

Stitchcraft also produced pattern books specifically for male garments.

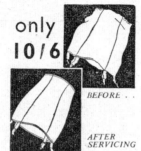

The corsets of Victorian and Edwardian times were long gone but women still liked a sturdy, boned foundation garment to give shape and support.

Since the sale of silk stockings was banned in late 1940, lisle stockings became popular. However, these were rationed so they were often repaired and darned using specialist sewing threads like this.

Lisle stockings were only available in various shades of brown and in 1941 there was a fashion for more cheerful, brightly coloured knitted stockings such as these from *Stitchcraft* in January 1941.

newspapers and government information sheets stated, 'Every man and woman who comes within the category usually called "manual workers" is covered,' and would entitle the bearer to purchase either three utility overalls, two and a half boiler suits, two and a half pairs of industrial safety boots, two cotton shirts or more than one pair of boots. This included farm labourers, miners and steel workers. Applications for the coupons had to be made through the worker's trade union or employer. It was intended that any deficits in the supplied coupons would be made up from the worker's own clothing allowance, but many joked about what they what they would do with half of a pair of working boots.

Austerity Measures

The Making of Civilian Clothing (Restrictions) Order was passed in March 1942. This limited the amount of cloth used in each garment.

For women there were also limits on the number of buttons and seams they could have. Pleats, ruching, embroidery, braid and lace were all banned in the production of dresses and blouses. Skirts were limited to three buttons, six seams, two box pleats and only one pocket. The width of belts, collars and sleeves was also heavily restricted. Only four buttons were allowed on a coat. All shoes were to have neither open toes nor heels higher than 2 inches. Men were restricted to single-breasted suits only and the following were banned in the production of men's clothes: slits or buttons on cuffs, flaps over pockets, turn ups, zips, elastic in waistbands and double shirt cuffs. The standard length of shirts was shortened. Belts on coats or leather or metal buttons were also not allowed. Jackets were to be cut shorter, pleated jacket backs were forbidden and trouser legs could be no more than 19 inches in circumference. Pyjama pockets and tail coats were not permitted because they were not considered essential or useful. The length of men's socks was restricted to 9 inches; this was one of the most unpopular austerity measures. No boys under thirteen could have long trousers.

It was claimed such economies as removing 2 inches from bottom of men's shirts and the elimination of double cuffs resulted in the saving of 4 million square yards of cotton a year.

CC41: The Utility Mark

Good quality cheap clothing remained scarce even after the introduction of clothes rationing so the Utility scheme was introduced with the aim of creating clothing and shoes from government controlled materials that would guarantee quality and value in fabric products and even furniture.

In 1942 the Board of Trade commissioned the Incorporated Society of London Fashion Designers to design a range of Utility clothing. The team allocated to the task included designers Norman Hartnell, Digby Morton, Hardy Amies, Bianca Mosca, Edward Molyneux, Elspeth Champcommunal, Peter Russell, Victor Stiebel and Charles Creed.

The result was thirty-two designs produced from four basic outlines, all incorporating the austerity measures. It was hoped that the use of top designers would ensure that Utility clothes were not seen as the 'uniform' that some feared. The Board of Trade were only too aware that the scheme would succeed only if women believed they would not end up in unattractive clothes or some sort of state uniform.

The symbol that would be attached to every garment or product made under the scheme had to be eye catching and the Board of Trade held a competition among design companies to create it, a competition won by Reginald Shipp of Hargreaves. Based on the letters and number CC41 (Civilian Clothing or Controlled Commodities Order 1941) it became known simply as 'The Cheeses' because the stylised circle letter Cs looked like round cheeses with a wedge cut out.

THE ABLE LABEL

... "able" because it gives you the ability to distinguish instantly between an article that is genuine and one that is not; between a 'Dayella' children's garment and one that *is said to be* 'Dayella'. Women ask for 'Dayella' because they know that this fine Utility fabric is made and guaranteed by the makers of 'Viyella', that genuine 'Dayella' garments are made only by the makers of 'Viyella', William Hollins & Co. Ltd., Nottingham. Before buying any fabric or children's garment as 'Dayella', take the simple precaution of asking to see THE ABLE LABEL!

'Dayella'
Regd.

Manufactured only by WILLIAM HOLLINS & CO., LTD., VIYELLA HOUSE, NOTTINGHAM.

The CC41 Mark guaranteed that a garment conformed to the government's Utility clothing restrictions and was seen as a promise of good quality.

All materials that would bear the Utility Mark had to pass strict tests to ensure value. Properties from colour fastness and shrinkage to waterproof qualities, the weave and weight of the fabric were controlled. It was also stipulated that colours were to be as vibrant as possible from limited dyes. Eventually, two thirds of the material available for civilian clothing during wartime went into the manufacture of Utility clothes.

The scheme received a mixed greeting from the public. People were glad there were government controls being placed on the quality, prices and availability of goods but the term 'Utility' seemed to carry a stigma of utilitarian style with it and the products were never considered as good as those available pre-war.

The end of clothes rationing in 1949 did not mean the end of Utility clothing. Instead, Utility clothing production was to increase to 80 per cent of total output, Utility footwear was already at 94 per cent and at the end of July 1949 maximum prices of Utility clothing were cut by 5 per cent. The Utility scheme finally ended in March 1952.

Make Do and Mend

In 1941 the Board of Trade worked with women's groups such as the Women's Institute and Townswomen's Guilds, who had already been holding clothing repair schemes and thrift classes across the country, to produce a paper discussing the possibilities for the best ways and means of making clothes last. This led to the creation of the national 'Make Do and Mend' Scheme in 1942 that aimed to encourage people to make their own clothes, remodel clothes, create new garments and accessories out of old ones and to mend damaged clothes to help save on clothes coupons and reduce consumption of fabrics.

The Ministry of Information produced the *Make Do and Mend* booklet for the Board of Trade in 1943. Available through any bookseller, it was pointed out in the publicity that the booklet 'does not tell you how to spend coupons but how to spend them wisely' and suggested further that it would enable readers to 'get the last possible ounce of wear out of all your clothes and belongings'. Practical advice included tips on storing clothes, keeping moths away, how to look after garments in short supply, the best ways to mend and patch things, laundering with soap economy in mind, renovation, unravelling and re-knitting. The *Make Do and Mend* booklet was an overnight success and sold half a million copies in the first two weeks it appeared on the shelves.

Above Left: Cover of the *Make Do and Mend* booklet issued by the Ministry of Information for the Board of Trade in 1943. It contained many useful tips on making clothes and household items last longer and was incredibly popular, selling half a million copies in the first two weeks.
Above Right: A bright and cheerful cover on a rationing theme for *Home Notes*, 5 August 1944.

This young lady photographed to advertise a Newcastle grocer's in 1943 embodies all things rationed. The carrier on the front of the bicycle holds the standard weekly rations for a family and she is wearing a Utility dress, to which she has added contrasting details to the collar and cuffs; her cardigan is of a sturdy cable knit but without the extravagance of a band around the bottom; and her shoes are plain, low-heeled lace-ups worn with home knitted ankle socks.

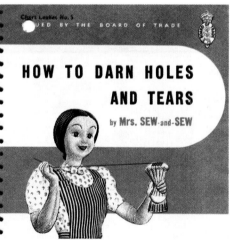

HOW TO DARN HOLES AND TEARS
by Mrs. SEW-and-SEW

Chart Leaflet No. 5
ISSUED BY THE BOARD OF TRADE

● Do not wait for holes to develop. It is better to darn as soon as garments begin to wear thin. Imitate, as well as possible, the texture of the fabric being darned. When darning a big hole, tack a piece of net at the back and darn across it, and this will give an extra support for the stitches. A tear should be tacked round on to a piece of paper, to hold the edges in position.

ISSUED BY THE BOARD OF TRADE

"Magpie Blouse"
by Mrs. SEW-and-SEW

"Piece your scrapbag oddments together to make a gay blouse like mine," Mrs. Sew-and-Sew suggests. "Choose a simple style without pleats or gathers—or, if you have no suitable pattern, go to a Make-do and Mend Class for help in cutting out."

Saves 5 coupons

HOW TO SET ABOUT IT. Trace blouse pattern on brown paper. Rule 2 stripes on this. Number these to match your colours, i.e., light (1), dark (2), print (3). Cut your strips, allowing ¼" turnings. Press in turnings. Pin strips to brown paper pattern, matching numbers on front, back and both sleeves. Tack and rule lines with tailor's chalk before machining. This helps to keep stitching straight. Seam up and finish off as usual.

Key to strip arrangement

See that back and 2nd sleeve match

★ Your local Evening Institute, Technical College or Women's Organisation is probably running a Make-Do and Mend Class near you. Ask at your Citizen's Advice Bureau.

The Board of Trade also devised Mrs Sew-and-Sew to be the face of the campaign and by mid-1943 she was appearing in nearly every magazine and newspaper, giving useful tips on repairing and caring for clothes.

By Oct 1942 there were between 800 and 900 Make Do and Mend groups and almost 1,000 coupon saving classes established across the country. Make Do and Mend fashion shows were staged and 'Mend for Victory' exhibitions toured the major towns and cities in England, Scotland and Wales.

The Board of Trade also devised the endearing Rag Doll character Mrs Sew-and-Sew as the 'face' of Make Do and Mend. By mid-1943 she appeared in nearly every magazine, cheerfully dispensing tips and advice on repairing and caring for clothes and encouraging women to attend Make Do and Mend classes run by local Women's Institutes and the Women's Voluntary Service. By 1944 Make Do and Mend had become a way of life in Britain.

Clothes for those with coupons to spend illustrated in *Home Notes* September 1945. Austerity and Utility clothing measures are still in force but the war has just ended. Styles are still simpler than those of pre-war years but hoped-for change is shown by voluminous sleeves, decorative bows, flared skirts and big patch pockets.

6

The Men and Women about Town

Be he on his way to work in an office, in a factory, in a trade, or out on the town, the garb of the average man on the street during the Second World War revolved around the two or three-piece suit. One, the old one, would be worn for work and the newer 'best' suit was for going out and special occasions, both usually in darker, conservative colours such as navy blue or shades of brown wool suit material or tweed. With shortages as they were, and bearing in mind that many people did not have the disposable income to keep buying clothes on a whim or changing fashions as they do today, the purchase of any garment would have been made with practicality in mind. In the late 1920s and throughout the 1930s pocket watches came to be seen as very old fashioned; the new vogue was for the wrist watch. Waistcoats, with their watch pockets synonymous with the display of the old-fashioned gold and silver Albert watch chains, were becoming less fashionable. Replacing them were the knitted V-neck sleeveless jumpers such as the multi-coloured Fair Isle associated with the more outdoors and adventurous types, especially when worn with

This photograph was taken in the early war years: there are still late 1930s fashions on show, with the long coats and dresses, but the two ladies on the right are wearing early 1940s suits.

a tweed jacket and lighter weight high-waisted trousers. Wartime economies soon meant that suits were made without waistcoats at all. Most men hung onto their pre-war suits in the early war years, reinforcing and renovating them as they went along, often using the old, worn-out suit waistcoats to patch and repair them. They took to wearing the knitted, sleeveless jumpers of various hues with their suit jacket and trousers, with maybe a new tie to add a dash of colour. Men in sharp cut, new double-breasted suits of the American style with wide lapels would attract the question 'Where did he get that?' and the answer would probably be the black market and he would be treated with some suspicion of being a 'wide boy' or 'spiv'.

In the days when the motto was, 'If you want to get ahead – Get a hat!' it was still rare to see a bare-headed man on the street. The cloth cap was still the demesne of the working man unless of obvious good quality, a generous wide cut and worn with tweeds for outdoor activities. The hat of choice for the British man about town during the war and for many years after was the

As the war carried on magazines were printed mainly in black and white, colour being saved for the front cover, as shown here with *Home Notes* from October 1944.

New slimline patterns for clothes, using less fabric and fewer embellishments, were produced under the Utility clothing regulation, 1944.

New Tunic Frocks and a Slim-line Coat
Ideas to help you when clothes-planning for colder days

trilby. As leather shortages tightened more and more men were wearing shoes for everyday wear rather than ankle boots.

Style for women during the war was often problematic due to shortages that soon kicked in after the outbreak of war, so the styles on the street from the late 1930s certainly lingered well into the early war years. Those able to buy or make their own clothes in the latest styles would aim for A-line, knee length skirts worn with a fitted jacket with padded shoulders and nipped-in waist. Coats and daytime dresses followed similar lines. As shortages became more acute skirts became shorter, for two main reasons: it would mean less fabric would be used in production of new items, and hems of older skirts would be turned up as they wore out. It was also argued that shorter skirts were more practical, particularly as many women had taken up cycling due to fuel shortages. Popular daywear included skirt suits in durable fabrics such as tweed or wool, dresses that could be worn in daytime and into the evening, twin sets, button-down and shirtwaist dresses, box coats and knitwear. Separates became popular as they allowed a mix and match variety in a limited wardrobe. Male clothing had a big impact on women's outerwear. Most

Above Left: Footwear during the war changed dramatically: heels became lower, shoes stouter and more functional. They had to be made to last as both leather and rubber became scarce as supplies were directed to military use. They might not be glamorous, but a good pair of stout shoes would be of more use than peep-toed evening shoes.

Above Right: Still seen as rather defiant in the early war years, one of the major changes in women's fashion during the war was the acceptance of trousers as an appropriate item of clothing for women to wear outside of the work environment.

popular were fly fronted gabardine raincoats, belted single-breasted coats and box coats in masculine styles feminised by cut.

The smartest suits had a military look with broad padded shoulders, straight fronts and moderately flared skirts with a pleat at the back. Shortages in cloth saw more women adopt knitted jumpers as part of their wardrobe essentials and a huge array of attractive, fashionable patterns were produced by companies like Sirdar and Bestway. Magazines such as *Stitchcraft* and *Home Notes* also became very popular, with their blend of fashion and style articles, knitting and fashion patterns and photographs of attractive, often smiling, models wearing the garments. Even in times of the greatest shortages when the magazines had to be produced half their normal size due to paper shortages, they maintained their attractive coloured covers that brought a very welcome spot of brightness and cheer to what otherwise would look like very dour rows of black and white magazines on news stands and coffee tables across the nation.

Trousers for women dated back to the First World War and had been worn for some outdoor pursuits in the years afterwards, but in the early years of the Second World War the slacks worn by younger women who enjoyed their practicality and comfort were also worn by the girls in the knowledge that they were still perceived by some as being a bit daring and even rebellious. As more women in the military were issued battledress trousers for their day-to-day work, and female drivers in the Civil Defence and emergency services

Late war style mirrored the active service uniforms and berets of the British fighting forces. This centre spread from *Home Notes* magazine, 1944, is selling patterns to make a fashionable battledress-style jacket from an old topcoat but also a skirt from old trousers and a blouse from an old shirt.

wore uniform trousers, they became far more accepted and a distinctive look of the later war years. By 1944 high wasted trousers, when worn with cropped jackets cut battledress style (this saved thousands of yards of material in production) worn with a sweater, stout shoes, tweed coat and a beret, became a highly fashionable look for both men and women from 1944 onwards. This look was in no small way a mirror of Britain's most prominent military officer, leader of the Desert Rats and one of the victors of D-Day, a real man of the moment who was seen as one who had led the turn in the tide of the war – Field Marshal Bernard Montgomery.

When it came to hats and headwear for women in wartime, practicality was the key. The wide brimmed felt hats of the 1930s, just like the clothes, lingered on through the war but soon became associated with older women or those in positions of authority. Ladies' trilbies and hats similar in silhouette to those worn by Greta Garbo became very popular, as did the beret later in the war. Film star Veronica Lake inspired the peek-a-boo hairstyle that became popular, and was just long enough to keep up and under control during the day, but which could be worn long for parties and social occasions. Women had used nets to keep their hair out of the way but the harder wartime work and shortages saw heavy

Above Left: This pretty young lady is sporting a typical hairstyle of the time: long enough to wear loose when going out, short enough to roll up at the back, out of the way, for work. The photograph is signed 'Fondest Love Muriel, July 1941.'

Above Right: The snood was a very popular way of holding longer hair away from the face. They could be heavy duty for work or lacy and elegant for the evening, and because it could be made at home, it proved a firm favourite throughout the war years.

BESTWAY LEAFLET No. 445

4 TURBANS, KNITTED & CROCHETED, and KNITTED GLOVES *on Two Needles*

3ᵈ

The popularity of the turban lasted through most of the decade. Here, Bestway offer both knitted and crocheted varieties. The turban was useful to keep hair out of the way but also, once shampoo and soap became difficult to get, they covered hair that may not be as clean as the wearer liked.

duty snoods become popular. These could be made at home and were extremely useful for keeping hair tied and out of the way. For the woman 'doing her bit' for the war effort in a host of jobs on the land, in the factories or canteens, the practical scarf turban became the iconic emblem of the hands-on woman war worker. Easy to make at home from scrap fabric, and eminently practical for war work, in truth it was also good for hiding unstyled hair and allowed the wearer to get off to work without such worries. In truth, it was also good for hiding unwashed hair as shampoo became scarce towards the end of the war.

Fuel shortages in 1943 resulted in people taking fewer baths and in any social situation body odour or 'B.O.' is really unpleasant; deodorants were the answer, but many women were wary. *The Lady* magazine of May 1943 stated: 'Some people are still nervous of deodorants, thinking they are harmful. Of course they are not. They are a vital necessity for your friend's sake as well as yours.'

So, what of going out for the evening? In times of shortages and rationing what was a girl to do? There was plenty of advice in the popular magazines about making new dresses if

For less than a **Pound**

This charming little dress, ideal for those special dates, costs, with long sleeves, 18/9; short sleeves, 18/4. Cut out ready to sew. Details opposite

CUT-OUT FROCK
32-40 in. busts

No. 2384 B

No. 2384 A

Dresses ideal for 'those special dates' for less than a pound, *Home Notes*, December 1945.

As in the First World War, many women wore sweetheart brooches in the form of the cap badge of their husband, sweetheart or brother's regiment. The picture above is an example of a winged Royal Air Force brooch.

for smart healthy Hair ..

Enlist

BRYLCREEM

THE PERFECT HAIR DRESSING

In handy Jars and Active Service Tubes **1/-**

Also bottles; 1/-, 1/6, 1/9, 2/6

County Perfumery Co., Ltd., North Circular Road, West Twyford, N.W.10

Men were not forgotten when it came to advertising. Brylcreem, for 'smart healthy hair', utilised the forces in their advertising campaigns. The service most associated with wearing it was the RAF – hence the nickname of 'the Brylcreem Boys'.

you could obtain the material or how to restyle old dresses to the latest styles, livening them up with colourful homemade accessories and embroidered embellishments.

Any woman wanting to show her thoughts were with her husband, son or a well-loved brother or to show her affection for a serviceman would wear (or in the latter case would often be given by said serviceman to wear) a 'sweetheart' brooch. Attractively made in gilded brass or plated metals, often enamelled, sometimes with a round mother of pearl backing, they would be attached by a brooch pin to the lapel or dress of the wearer. Each badge would be a small version of the regimental cap badge, Navy insignia or RAF wings of the wearer's loved one.

Make-up was never rationed because it was feared it would have severely damaged female morale. The Board of Trade deemed cosmetics an essential requirement and tried to keep basics such as mascara and lipstick always available. However, that did not mean they were in plentiful supply or always at reasonable prices and by 1942 the supply of beauty products had fallen to less than 25 per cent of the 1938 level. The problem was that adverts and fashion articles in magazine and newspapers constantly reinforced the idea that beauty was a woman's responsibility to keep up morale. With the lack of available cosmetics in mind they also inspired women to become inventive with such advice as: Collect the stubs of lipstick, melt them down, mix together and pour into a small pot to reuse once solid. If mixed with a spot of cold cream the lipstick would go further and could also be used as rouge. Beetroot juice sealed with petroleum jelly or solid rouge could be used to tint the lips. Use lard instead of cold

What was right in Beauty yesterday is wrong to=day—the way you wear your clothes, the way you do your hair, make= up your mouth, display your nails— here are up=to=the=minute notes

B Y

J A N E   C L A R E

V necks, low square necks, and heart shapes are all coming into the picture now—it's good-bye to close, round necklines. Your face is round and your neck short? Then this is your chance to slim your dress-lines, and improve your looks. Deep, narrow V necks are the most becoming of all, as you can see.

Lips have been all sorts of shapes the last few years— the sultry belle look is right out now. The most common lipstick fault is blurred, ending-in-nothing effect. Smart girls, now, apply their lipstick to follow the natural lines, with clearly defined edges everywhere—It's up to you !

Long, claw-like nails are very much pre-war! They break easily and are impossible to keep nicely groomed now that nail varnish is so hard to obtain. File your nails down to a smooth, rounded oval (not too far down into the corners), that repeats the oval of your fingertips.

Blue-pencilled by all beauty experts is the little girl hair-do—it's still seen, but the new line for hair is a clean, sculptured one that shows the shape of the head. The back hair is turned into one neat roll, or a series of flat pin curls— or the hair is cut to a new version of the semi-shingle with the hair brushed across.

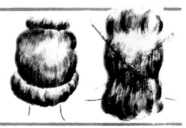

In war as in peace, some of the most popular women's magazine features showed the latest trends in clothing styles, ways to wear your hair and apply your make-up.

Cosmetics firms often used glamorous images to advertise goods, a reminder that good times were possible in all circumstances, even during war. After all, what woman would not want to dance in the arms of a handsome RAF officer while wearing a flowing evening gown scented with 'Evening in Paris'?

cream and make up remover. Powdered starch makes a good substitute for face powder. Use moustache wax, boot polish and burnt cork in place of mascara. Gravy browning, walnut juice, tea, brown shoe polish and iodine were all tried to colour legs in the absence of stockings; there were even special products advertised as: 'Those exciting new stockings which come out of a bottle. You can buy this leg make up in two shades Grape Mist and Gold Mist ... you can paint about 8 pairs of stockings from the 1/3d bottle.'

7
Wartime Weddings

The white wedding was firmly established as 'the done thing' over the years after the First World War. On the outbreak of war in September 1939, the do it now or never spirit caught the imaginations of many couples and there was an upsurge in weddings. Statistics showed Warwickshire topped the wedding list for the quarter ending 30 September with 6,889, closely followed by Staffordshire with 5,188, Gloucestershire with 3,219, Worcestershire with 1,525, Shropshire with 765 and Herefordshire with 350. The Sheffield registry office recorded eighty couples married in one day.

At the start of the war there were still formal weddings with men in morning suits and bridesmaids in pastel colours but as more men joined the services it became acceptable for them to wear their uniform. The introduction of purchase tax in October 1940 and clothes rationing in 1941 affected bridal choices. Wedding dresses were still available to buy but rationing made this difficult; they used a lot of clothing coupons and there were often

In this photograph taken c. 1943, this bride wears a dress that can be worn on other occasions while the groom (a lance-corporal in the Army Catering Corps) and best man are in uniform. The bridesmaids are probably wearing their best dresses. Few people had coupons to spare for wedding clothes.

Above Left: A Royal Artillery bombardier and his bride, *c.* 1941. The bride wears a suit with a plain skirt but a fancy jacket that may well have been adapted from a pre-war outfit. Short crochet gloves were a popular accessory.

Above Right: A young Royal Navy telegraphist and his bride, Barnsley, South Yorkshire, *c.* 1943. While he is in uniform, his bride wears a Utility suit and blouse and a simple hat decorated with net. Her sandals are most likely pre-war, being strappy and open toed.

waiting lists of several months. From 1941 white weddings became the exception rather than the rule but were not impossible, especially when a little initiative was used.

Curtain lace was exempt from the rationing points system and was often used to make a veil and a long lace overdress worn over a nightdress, making a lovely wedding gown. There was generally little fabric to work with so the bodice would be fitted with a V shaped, square or heart shaped neckline, long, tight fitted sleeves puffed or padded at the shoulder and the skirt narrow and without a train. Furnishing fabrics and lace were also used as they were exempt from coupons.

Fresh flowers became scarce and expensive so bouquets of perfumed paper and linen flowers were commonly carried by the bride and a homemade card horseshoe painted silver or covered in silver paper suspended on a ribbon was a common addition to bring good luck.

It was not unusual for 'borrowed plumes' to be worn at weddings, even in peacetime, but war made the practice far more prevalent than ever as brides wore their mother's or grandmother's dress to wed. In some towns and communities a few pre-war white wedding dresses were used for a number of marriages if the women were all of a similar size: with a dart here, let out there and turn or a drop of a hem made, the dress was just right.

A young RAF corporal and his bride, 1939. The amount of fabric in the bride's dress reflects a time before coupons, restrictions and Utility clothes.

As shortages hit harder and life moved at a faster pace in wartime, weddings became far more spontaneous and hastily arranged as often the groom was soon to depart for war service or only had a limited leave of absence granted. It was not unusual for the groom, best man and bridesmaid's clothes to be borrowed. Some couples opted to buy new clothes for their wedding that could be used afterwards for everyday wear. It was common to see the groom wearing his uniform and the bride in her new Utility suit with straight skirt and semi fitted jacket with padded shoulders, a small hat perched well forward, a spray of flowers pinned to the lapel and a pair of crocheted gloves to finish off the ensemble.

Barbara Cartland was moved by the situation of girls having to get married without a proper wedding dress and organised the first of a number of 'pools' of second hand wedding dresses around the country. In 1943 Mrs George Shaw Green of Dayton, Ohio, presented five white wedding gowns because 'she wanted some of the Service women of Britain to have the romance of a white wedding in spite of coupons and clothes economy'. Four other dresses were also donated, all through the British War Relief Society of the USA. The gowns were

JUNE WEDDING

Adorable Designs
for the Summer
Bride and her
Small Attendant

Pattern
particulars
opposite

Child's Frock and Bonnet No. 11,212 2-8 years.   Bride's Gown No. 11,209, 32-40 in. busts

This 1944 magazine advert for a wedding dress pattern, although the dress still has simple lines, assumes the bride, her family and friends can obtain enough material for the long flared skirt and the ground-length veil.

borrowed at a charge of 10s for cleaning. No alterations were allowed except for the turning up of hems. This was followed by a similar gesture by Eleanor Roosevelt, who organised a collection of dresses and veils from American brides that were sent to Britain for loan to servicewomen to get married in.

The use of the white silk from fallen parachutes was illegal during wartime. Officially, if a parachute was found it should be turned in to the authorities but parachute silk could be obtained on the black market or from 'a friend of a friend' on one of the rescue crews and it was used to make wedding dresses. If their piece was big enough, they could make a couple of pairs of French knickers from the left-over material. After the end of the war, surplus RAF parachutes were offered for sale whole or in 11ft/3.35m triangular panels, coupon free.

As the war went on, many women also joined either military or Home Front services. Both bride and groom often wore their uniforms and had guards of honour holding an array of objects aloft, from the formal drawn swords of brother officers in the military services to the likes of axes for firemen, splints for ambulance and rescue workers, ladles for canteen workers

Wedding group, Keswick, Cumbria, August 1944. The bride is probably wearing a borrowed wedding dress from the late 1930s; the veil is certainly too long to be wartime. The men are also wearing older double-breasted suits.

A wedding group showing a Royal Navy gunner and his bride, c. 1944. The bride is wearing a 1930s dress and her bridesmaids are wearing matching outfits, something they would have had to work at together as a team of family and friends to achieve at this late stage in the war.

and even long loaves of bread for cook-house staff to form an arch as the happy couple left the church. They were not perfect events but still, for many, it would be remembered as the happiest day of their lives in marriages that endured for fifty, sixty and even more years afterwards.

8
The New Look

The end of the war in 1945 did not see an immediate end to rationing. In fact, as men began to return home rationing was increased and it soon became apparent the post-war years would be times of austerity. However, it was certainly noticeable that there were unprecedented numbers of well-dressed men on the streets in new suits. The suits were issued to all personnel leaving the armed services having served their term; in other words, they were demobilized or 'demobbed' and the 'demob suit' became a phenomenon on the streets of post-war Britain. Cut in a number of standard designs and materials, men were offered a choice of a double-breasted pinstriped three-piece suit or a single-breasted jacket and flannel trousers, felt hat or flat cap, two shirts, a tie, laced leather Oxford or Derby shoes and a raincoat. Both double and single-breasted suits had flapped side pockets,

The war has been over less than a month and rationing is still in place. Magazines, such as this edition of *Home Chat* of 29 September 1945, produced patterns for more extravagant clothing in anticipation of an end to rationing. They were not to know that it would continue till February 1949.

Throughout the war you could often find patriotic motifs incorporated into clothing. There was even a fad for a 'Victory' jumper in 1942, knitted with contrasting columns of Vs. Here we have buttons in red, white and blue with the V symbol as well as a felted Victory pin and ribbon worn on the lapel to celebrate victory and an end to hostilities in 1945.

buttons on cuffs and an outside breast pocket. Generally produced in good quality material and well made, they were, however, mass produced, unadventurous and very much 'off the peg'. They were criticised for being skimpy in size and somewhat ill-fitting, hardly the suit for one who had given his all in war, but as many of the lads said, it was better than nothing.

Wartime regulations had a very positive effect on the manufacturing industry. As a result of staff shortages and reduced facilities, new time-saving equipment was developed along with huge improvements in mass production. Methods of cutting, sizing and fitting improved greatly and carried on after the war, but it would be years before the clothing market would be ration free or anything like it was before the war. With clothing still subject to rationing, many men turned to the vast amounts of Government surplus uniforms available from all three services as well as old ARP boiler suits that made great workwear. These garments were flooding the market and, best of all, because they were

Interior photograph of the ladies' underwear department in Blaylocks, Newcastle, 1946. The clothing on offer and that worn by the customers is still Utilitarian. There was no immediate end to the scarcities of war and women carried on wearing their wartime clothing well into the end of the decade.

With the war over, embellishments on clothing could once again become commonplace. This Bestways catalogue from the late 1940s re-introduces the dressmaker to the joys of smocking.

Still times of rationing and restrictions at the dressmaking and tailoring department of Blaylocks, Newcastle, 1946.

in effect second hand, even if never worn, they were coupon free! From 1946 the choice of available fabrics gradually became larger and traditional materials returned to the market, initially for export. They were later joined by nylon and other new synthetics. Women cheered when nylon stockings were produced in the UK again in December 1946. Silk stockings would not reappear on the open market again until 1948 but the price was an inhibitive 23s a pair.

Meanwhile, liberated Paris resumed its place at the centre of the fashion world again, and on 12 February 1947 the first exhibition of Christian Dior's 'Corolla' line took place at 30 Avenue Montaigne. The designs were a total contrast to the war years: skirts were very full and almost ankle length, waists were once again nipped in with 'waspie' corsets, hips and busts were padded, shoulders were rounded and there were layers of petticoats. Jackets were figure hugging and there was a mass of pleats, tucks, trims and other fripperies not seen during the war. It was a style condemned by some as too extravagant but it was a style and a silhouette that embodied a new, unfettered post-war world of fashion, and a style that would become known simply as the 'New Look'.

Princess Margaret wore a New Look coat for her parents' Silver Wedding in April 1948. Reports took pains to point out it had not been made from scratch but altered to the design by Norman Hartnell. Even princesses were bound by the rules in Austerity Britain.

Utility at its best

Outstanding Values in the
Lovely Summer Collection
AT

BONDS

"PAMELA"

"WENDY"

"BETTY"

"WENDY" One of the five styles in striped rayon pique which includes :
High neck-line with full un-pressed pleated skirt. Red Green, Blue, 36-42 **76/6**

Very full skirt with square neck, buttoned to waist. Red, Green, Blue, 36-42 **81/11**

High round neck with pleated basque. Fastening at back, 36-42. **76/6**

Flared skirt with hip pockets, V. neck-line. Buttoned to waist, 36-42 **76/6**

"PAMELA" Cool and attractive in floral printed art silk, featuring the new neckline. Variety of colours! Stock sizes. **59/11**

" BETTY ". Floral printed spun with attractive flared skirt, button front to waist, short sleeves. Sizes 36-44 in. **19/11**

Limited quantity of Linen Effect Printed Rayon, Button through style with pockets, 38 in. and 40 in. only. Blue, Green, Pink **39/11**

BONDS (NORWICH LTD.) ALL SAINTS GREEN

The Utility scheme did not end till March 1952. However, the post-war Utility clothing attempted to keep up with new fashions. This advert for Bonds in Norwich shows Utility dresses based on Dior's 'New Look', which made its first appearance in 1947.

The extravagances of the 'New Look' were not possible in post-war Britain. The British clothing industry toned down the look and made more affordable garments in the New Look style, such as the coat on the right, in 1949.

Sadly, Britain was still stuck in the mire of clothes rationing and British designers had no other option than to innovate ways to imitate the look in order for it to comply with restrictive clothing regulations. Consequently, they produced an A-line skirt that provided the same look without the excessive yardages of fabric (some of Dior's catwalk creations required 18 meters of fabric). These modified versions began to appear in department stores in late 1947 and by 1949 most shops were selling what were more commonly called the 'ballerina' skirts in Britain.

The return to perceived normality for the British clothing industry would take longer than anticipated. It was not until April 1949, in fact, that Harold Wilson, the then President of the Board of Trade, announced an end to clothes rationing, but even then financial limitations and lack of available material did not see a vast array of clothes flood the market, and the fashion industry would bloom in elegance and style, some would argue for the last time, in the 1950s.

9
What Now?

Getting involved

Membership of a society is not essential to learning more about the fashions of any period, but it can be a great way to make contacts, find out about special exhibitions and events or other ways you can get involved. Many museums have their own costume and textile groups and there is the Costume Society, which promotes the study of all aspects of clothing and textiles with the primary aim of encouraging access to costume history of all periods. http://www.costumesociety.org.uk/

An advert for Bestway paper patterns from September 1949. The longer, fuller skirts and fitted bodices that would become the hallmark style of the next decade are already becoming apparent in these designs.

Collecting

One of the best ways to develop an interest in any subject is to collect books, journals and magazines, photographs and ephemera relating to it. Now, be warned that this can become addictive – there will always be 'just one more' volume to join the others – but it is still a hobby that can be within most people's pocket and it can also be very enjoyable and a constant journey of discovery over many years to come. When starting out, we suggest the books in the reading list would be helpful. They are well illustrated and should enable anyone with a new-found interest in 1940s fashion to start finding out more about it and finding the areas of the subject that really interest them.

Many people soon find they would like to own some original 1940s garments of their own and it is still possible for that to be achieved. There are some superb vintage clothing fairs around the UK but be prepared that the most common sizes you will encounter in the original clothing on offer are small by our modern standards. There are also pitfalls to look for such as clothing that has been reproduced or converted to look 1940s for re-enactors, and please also make sure it has not suffered an attack from moths, which can, if unchecked, spread to your other clothes. Be aware that American clothes from the 1940s that are often offered via online auction houses, no matter how attractive they may be, would not have been common sights on British streets, and although they may be tempting and 'of the period', they will not give you the classic look of the British 1940s. Read and enjoy well-illustrated books and take the time to find out the long established and respected traders at the fairs; there are good reasons for why they have been around for so long. Don't let your heart rule your head; just because you like a garment, if it isn't quite right for British 1940s style, that will never make it right. Never feel pressured to buy an item. Save your money for the real deal or get an authentic British pattern (these are now reproduced by the major dress making pattern companies) and suitable material and get it made or even sew it or knit it yourself.

Further Reading

Adie, Kate, *Corsets to Camouflage* (Hodder & Stoughton, 2003).

Brown, Mike, *CC41 Utility Clothing* (Sabrestorm, 2014).

Brown, Mike, *The 1940s Look, Recreating The Fashions, Hairstyles and Make-up of the Second World War* (Sabrestorm, 2009).

Dirix, Emmanuelle and Fiell, Charlotte, *1940s Fashion The Definitive Sourcebook* (Goodman Fiell, 2013).

Fogg, Marnie, *Vintage Fashion Knitwear, Collecting and Wearing Designer Classics* (Carlton Books, 2010).

Ewing, Elizabeth, *History of 20th Century Fashion* (Batsford, 2008).

Hashagen, Joanna, *Wedding Dresses from the Bowes Museum* (Friends of the Bowes Museum, 2003).

Kenett, Frances, *The Collectors Book of Twentieth Century Fashion* (HarperCollins Publishers Ltd, 1983).

Lansdell, Avril, *Wedding Fashions 1860–1980* (Shire Publications Ltd, 1986).

Laughton Mathews, Vera, *Blue Tapestry* (Hollis & Carter, 1949).

Shrimpton, Jayne, *Fashion in the 1940s* (Shire, 2016).

Storey, Neil R., *Family Military Photographs and How to Date Them* (Countryside, 2009).

Storey, Neil R. and Housego, Molly, *Women in the Second World War* (Shire, 2011).

Storey, Neil R. and Kay, Fiona, *The Home Front in World War Two* (Amberley, 2017).

Summers, Julie, *Fashion on the Ration* (Profile, 2016).

Walford, Jonathan, *Forties Fashion from Siren Suits to the New Look* (Thames & Hudson, 2008).

Waller, Jane & Vaughan-Rees, Michael, *Women in Wartime: The Role of Women's Magazines 1939–1945* (Macdonald & Co. (Publishers) Ltd, 1990).

Places to visit

There are a numerous fashion and textile museums around the country; it is worthwhile looking them up but don't forget to see what the museums on your doorstep have to offer as many of them will have small permanent displays of 1940s life and fashions. It's also worth looking online to see what temporary exhibitions are being staged at some of the larger museums each year.

Imperial War Museum, Lambeth Road, London SE1 6HZ

Established at the end of the First World War as Britain's National War Museum, it's always a great place to start your journey in learning about life and fashions in the Second World War.

Imperial War Museum (North), The Quays, Trafford Wharf Road, Manchester, M17 1TZ

IWM (North) has powerful displays exploring how war affects people's lives through a good selection of displays covering a variety of aspects of the Second World War and regularly stages temporary exhibitions.

The Victoria and Albert Museum, Cromwell Road, London SW7 2RL

Spanning five centuries, the V&A fashion collection is the largest and most comprehensive in the world. www.vam.ac.uk/collections/fashion

The Fashion Museum, Bath, houses one of the world'd greatest museum collections of historic and fashionable dress. www.fashionmuseum.co.uk/

The Harris Museum, Art Gallery and Library, Market Square, Preston, Lancashire PR1 2PP

The Harris Museum is a very good example of a well presented and accessible provincial costume collection that reflects local manufacturers and clothes worn by local people from the seventeenth century up to modern times. http://www.harrismuseum.org.uk/collections/119-costume-textile

Web Resources

www.iwm.org.uk/collections

Imperial War Museum collections is a superb resource for both photographs and memorabilia research relating to both the fighting forces and the Home Front in two World Wars. Explore the whole IWM sites for events, special exhibitions and other connections.

www.nationalarchives.gov.uk/help-with-your-research/research-guides/second-world-war/

The National Archives offers a vast resource for anyone researching life, wartime organisations, businesses and Government policies on the British Home Front with your research/research guides.

www.bbc.co.uk/history/ww2peopleswar/

WW2 People's War is an online archive of Second World War memories written by the public, gathered by the BBC.

LITTLE BLACK FROCK

It's the standby of
every smart girl
and this model is
especially attract-
ive—with two de-
tachable fronts to
ring the changes

This Two-Way Frock with detach-
able fronts is Pattern No. 11,783,
A and B, and is cut in 32-40 inch
bust sizes. It costs 1s. 6d., plus
1d. postage, from "Home Notes"
Pattern Shop, Tower House,
Southampton St., London, W.C.2.

The 'Little Black Frock' from *Home Notes*, 1944.